VOYAGE TO VICTORY

The Voice of a Sailor
in the Pacific
1943-1945

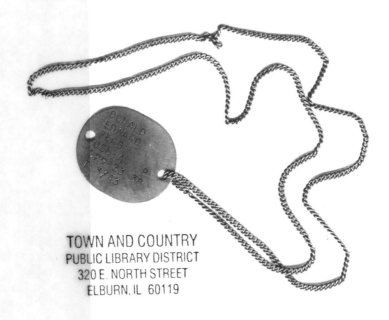

Susan Berg Heeg

Based on the letters of
Donald Edward Berg

River Road Publications, Inc. Spring Lake, Michigan, USA

Dedicated to David Heeg:
My husband, my support,
my heart.
I am thankful for you every day!

Library of Congress Control Number: 2004092097

ISBN: 0-938682-79-2

Printed in the United States of America

CONTENTS

In memory of Dad:
A man of few words,
who must have used them all up
in letters during the war;
A man who lived what he said
and loved his family;
A man loved and remembered.

INTRODUCTION

Realizing that duty to his country was important, Donald Edward Berg, my father, was just
seventeen years of age when he enlisted in the
U.S. Navy and left for boot camp. It was January
1943, just before his eighteenth birthday. Boot
camp helped him grow up, and navy school in
Jefferson City, Missouri, and at Navy Pier in
Chicago, Illinois, prepared him for his tour of
duty. He trained as a Motor Machinist Mate 2nd
Class and joined the crew of the USS *Pakana*
(ATF 108), a tugboat, in October 1943.

The *Pakana* ("The Mighty P" as my dad called
it) was commissioned on December 17, 1943.
After shore duty along our Pacific coast, the
Pakana left for Pearl Harbor in March 1944. The
crew spent 1944 and 1945 helping sailors and
ships in distress and in salvage work throughout
the Pacific, including the Marshall Islands, Guam,
Okinawa, the Philippine Islands, Saipan, and
Nagasaki. On January 2, 1946, my father left the
Pakana and eventually boarded the USS
Ticonderoga for the U.S.A. and home. He was not
yet 21 years old, and he had seen so much!

Throughout his preparations for war and
during his tour of duty in the Pacific, my dad was
as every sailor, holding on to three things: his
God, his family, and his fellow crew members. At
home in Minneapolis, Minnesota, his family, like

families all over the United States, prayed and wrote letters of encouragement and of news from home. My dad placed his family on a rotation of letter writing and almost every other day wrote to one of them: his mom, his pop, his sister Marguerite (age fifteen when Dad left home), brother John (twin to Marg), and sister Eleanor (twelve years old when Dad went to boot camp). He also wrote to his older brother, Herbert, who was serving with the First Army in Europe. My grandma saved these letters, and I read them for the first time after my dad passed away in June of 1996. They are filled with first-hand information

Herbert, John, Pop
Marg, Ellie, Mom

about what life was like for sailors in the World War II years from 1943 to 1945. Descriptions of everyday life, from a sailor's perspective, place you in boot camp, at navy school, and on the USS *Pakana* throughout a tour of duty in the Pacific. Censors kept him from telling all of his experiences, but when the censorship was lifted, the retelling of some events in later letters gives a sense of battle. Some letters take you into Nagasaki after the atomic bomb has been exploded. The eyewitness accounts are undoubtedly helpful in study of the Pacific war.

The greatest gifts in these letters, however, are the feelings and the love of family which come through. It was the contact with his family through these letters that kept my dad going in the toughest times of his life. His concern for his family comes across when he realizes how families are sacrificing during rationing. It was the little things of home which he missed so much and wanted his younger brother and sisters to appreciate.

My dad's voice in these letters is the voice of one, and yet many, who served in the Pacific during World War II. His experience was unique, and yet similar to all young men who answer the call in service to our country. Don Berg was fortunate that he was one who did make it home to all he loved. He would be the first to dedicate these letters to all of those in World War II who died for their country. War made him realize what truly counted: his God, his family, his friends in the service and at home, and the true joy of living in simple moments—moments of milk, ice cream, swimming, pictures, letters, fresh air, and laughter. I have not included all of my dad's letters, but perhaps by reading some of them, you too will have a new sense of what is truly important in life.

Susan Berg Heeg
Daughter of Donald Edward Berg

UNITED STATES NAVY

Dear mom, Pop, John, mary and Eleanor

Past Valley City a while ago. Kinda bumpy riding and it's hard to write. We didn't leave the station until 11:30 last night. Wow! is this train bumpy. We are traveling first class in a Pullman car. Didn't sleep much last night, too bumpy. The Porter called "hit the deck" a 6:00 and we ate about 7:00. Not doing much know, reading comic books. Boy did that coffee taste terrible this morning.

Written by hand.
your son
Donald

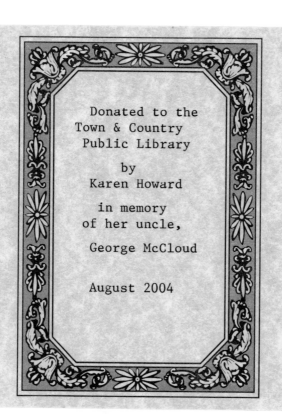

1
BOOT CAMP

In all branches of the armed forces, young enlisted or drafted men and women leave home to attend boot camps, which are located all over the United States. During boot camp, the recruits are given basic training and conditioning, and they are instilled with the principles on which the service is built.

During World War II, boot camp was also a time when young men realized that their lives in the armed forces would be quite different than in civilian life. Their schedules and behaviors were regulated by the officers in the camps. There was a benefit, however. While the civilian population of the United States was rationing everything from sugar to shoes, these new recruits were enjoying all the food necessary to build their strength and develop the fine fighting force which would eventually win the war. Donald Berg attended boot camp at Farragut, Idaho. Boot camp, however, was just a taste of what the future had in store.

Jan. 7, 1943

Dear Mom, Pop, John, Marg, and Eleanor,

Passed Valley City awhile ago. Kinda bumpy riding, and it's hard to write. We didn't leave the station until 11:30 last night. Wow!...is this train bumpy! We are traveling first class in a Pullman car. Didn't sleep much last night, too bumpy. The porter called "hit the deck" at 6:00, and we ate about 7:00. Not doing much now...reading comic books. Boy, did that coffee taste terrible this morning!

Written by hand,

Your son,

Donald

Jan. 10, 1943

Dear Mom,

Well, I am finally here in boot camp, but right now I don't feel so hot. We got our uniforms yesterday and with it.., two shots and a vaccination. My arms ached all evening and night. I had to stand watch last night from 2:00 until 4:00. This ruins the night for sleeping, because we have to get up at 5:30.

The trip out wasn't so bad, but it was awful slow. We thought we would never get here. After we got off the train, we went by bus to the camp. There we had to throw away all bottles with liquid in them, so I lost my hair oil. The next day we went to the physical examination and clothing building. Here we had another physical. They almost didn't pass me, because I used to walk in my sleep. After the physical, we rolled up the clothes to be sent home. The hangers are coming back, because we don't hang our clothes up. It's all rolled and placed in our sea bag. We got our clothes after our physical and boy, did we get a lot of it. It weighed a ton. After we got back to our barracks, we worked the rest of the afternoon rolling clothes. I was one of the men selected for guard duty. My time was from 2:00 to 4:00 in the morning. The one good thing about mine was that I was inside. The food is

O.K., but I still don't like beans for breakfast. We get beans three times a week.

Can you send me some shaving cream, because every man out here has to shave whether you have to or not.

We can't leave our barracks, because the whole company has been quarantined for scarlet fever. The only time we can go out is to eat or when on guard duty. We don't get out until Jan. 30.

Your son,

Donald

F-7 Barracks Interior

Our barracks here at Farragut

January 12, 1943

Dear Pop:

Well, we're starting to work harder every day. We did quite a bit of marching today out on the "Grinder". That's the Navy drill field. We did a lot of double time marching, which, if you lift your knees, is quite tiring. This morning we had our first inspection by the C.P.O., and he found plenty wrong. The reason for the inspection was that the 14th Battalion Commander, Lt. Fossette, wanted to inspect the barracks. We spent all day yesterday cleaning windows, scrubbing the deck, moving bunks, and sweeping the floors. Because the floors, or decks as we call them, were wet, we were moving bunks in our bare feet. Man, those bunks really flatten out your feet!

We're the bunch in Camp Hill that is always getting it in the neck. For breakfast, lunch, and supper we're always way too late or way too early. If we're early, we either have to stand around and wait or march around, and if we're late, we catch it at the mess hall.

The quarantine that is on the barracks is either going to be a break for us or a big setback. The C.P.O. said we might be placed on regular schedule in a day or two. If this happens we will be about a week ahead. Otherwise we will have to wait until the quarantine is lifted, which will be about Jan. 30, before we start our regular work. Our time isn't counted until we start regular work.

The other night a "gold braid" came in about 9:00 to check over the barracks and found waste paper in the G.I. can and a package of "Lucky Strikes" on a table. When he saw them, he almost blew his top. Worse yet was the fact that when he came back later, the G.I. can had more rubbish in it. This morning we got a lecture.

We've got a fairly good company, but there are a few lazy ones in it. We have 118 men in our Co. Most of the men are from Minnesota, Colorado, and California. The men from Minnesota are the best. Some of the men from California look like they haven't had a haircut for years. Every man out here that has his hair cut calls us "barber bait". We won't get our hair cut until we get out of quarantine, I think.

The only name you hear around here is "Hey, Mac". Every man in camp is called "Mac".

The food served here is darn good, better than the Army anyhow. We get plenty of meat, good dessert, milk once a week, coffee the rest of the time. Phooey on coffee!

Your son,

Donald

Getting Navy haircuts

Dear John:

No longer am I "barber bait". They just cut it off "buzz saw" style. It's a cut something like Don Strate's but worse. It isn't even, and it's too long.

You folks at home might like to know what we do all day, so I will write out a day's work. This morning at 5:00 we got up. Had a half hour to clean up ourselves and our bunks. At 6:00 we started to clean barracks. We had to move all the bunks, mop the floor, rearrange bunks, clean windows, and dust. We're upstairs in the barracks and have 118 men in our company. Clean up took about an hour and fifteen minutes. Then we lined up outside and marched over to the mess hall. This morning we had corn flakes, Navy hash, bread and butter, two oranges, and coffee. We generally eat between 7:15 and 7:30. After breakfast we came back to the barracks. We stayed there until 8:15. Then we went out on the Grinder and practiced marching. We marched until 10:00. Then we came back to barracks and cleaned up again. Right now, we won't have anything to do until lunch.

We're supposed to get our first $5.00 of our $50.00 in a day or two. I don't believe we get the lump sum until after graduation. Graduation will be from 7 - 15 weeks from now depending on how fast we advance.

Yesterday we all took out insurance. I took out $10,000 worth. Made it out to Mom.

How is the war going? We haven't heard a thing since we hit camp. We don't get a chance to leave the barracks.

The camp out here is different than you might think. It's not warm. There is snow... not too much, but enough. Weather is damp, and almost everyone in our barracks has a cold. It is funny though. You have a cold, but you don't feel sick. Out here you never see the sun. The guys say they have seen the sun 3 times in the last 2 months.

At 12:30 we went to lunch and had mashed potatoes, chicken on toast, chopped lettuce, bread and butter, and two pieces of cake. Boy, did it taste good. There is one thing we don't have to worry about.... That's sugar.

F-6 Mess Hall

Our mess hall

We have all we want. Just keep pouring it on!

    We went to supper at 5:30 and had, well, I don't know yet. I have been writing this letter in shifts. This afternoon we marched after lunch for a little over an hour. This morning the air was fairly cold, but around 12:00 it started to melt and when we went out, it was awful sloppy out. We were given the rest of the afternoon off to study the eleven rules of a sentry and the first five chapters of the BlueJacket's Manual. Time goes fairly fast out here, but at times when we don't have anything to do, it goes perty slow.

    A lot of the men here don't like to sit around and do nothing. They're all waiting for their first liberty. I think they will be disappointed as to how much they will get out of it.

    There are a few men here that are perty smart, but several of them are plenty dumb. Most of them joined the Navy to get out of having to work, but they have found out different.

Because of the quarantine, we can't go to the ship store. Thus everybody is short. When we came into camp, many men lost their stationary, so everybody has been bumming it off of me.

Out here most of the men are complaining about not getting enough sleep, but I have caught up on mine, and now I wake up a lot during the night.

Well, tonight it happened. We saw the sun. It had thawed all day, and the sun came out just as it was going down. The clouds cleared up, and you could see a long ways. All you could see was mountains.

Last night I washed my first clothes. Did a perty good job too. They had to be hung outside, so they didn't dry very well. I washed a bed sheet and handkerchief tonight.

For supper we had mashed potatoes, about 10 slices of fried sausage, a lima bean and beans dish, bread and butter, and an apple dessert something like Brown Betty. Tonight we're free to do anything we want inside the barracks until work detail. After that, we're free until 9:00. Then we have to be in bed.

Your brother,
Donald

Doing our laundry

Company clotheslines

Feb. 11, 1943

Dear Pop:

Well, this morning we got up at 5:30 and had to have our bunks made and cleaned up by 6:00. It doesn't seem bad getting up that early, but if I would have had to have done it before I joined, it would have been terrible. From 6 to 6:30, we cleaned the barracks. Then at 6:30 we went to chow. We had to be back by 7:35 to go

11

to colors in the drill hall. It's really a big drill hall about the size of the field house at the University of Minnesota. After the marching we went swimming for about five minutes to prove we could swim. There are 32 men that can't swim, and they won't get a liberty until they can swim at least 50 yards. After swimming, we went back to the barracks for a study session of the bluejacket's manual. After lunch we fell out for the rifle drill. We marched around two areas a distance of about two miles, and when we got back to the drill hall, those rifles felt like they weighed 50 pounds.

I read about rationing in the paper that coffee has to last six weeks. How is ours holding out? Are shoes rationed in Minnesota too?

Your son,
Donald

Farragut Naval Training Center drill hall

Swimming lessons at Farragut

Feb. 13, 1943

Dear John:

    We had our first captain's inspection this morning. I stood so long at parade rest and attention that my feet became numb. We got up at 4:45 this morning and cleaned up. Everyone put on clean clothes except a couple that caught it at inspection. We all changed pillow cases and mattress sheets. After that, all the boys were down shining shoes. Last night everyone scrubbed his leggings and underclothes. They had to be clean for today. At 8:30 we marched over to the drill hall and then removed our coats and lined up for inspection. The C.P.O. worked us for about a half hour. Then for about an hour and

a half, we stood at attention or parade rest.
When the inspecting officer came by, I stood at
the most rigid attention I have ever stood at.
After the inspecting officer had gone to the next
battalion, we were put at ease. When the men
moved, their joints cracked! During inspection,
there were about seven men in our company that
passed out. One man wasn't caught as he fell,
and he bounced off the floor. When he hit, it
sounded as though he was going through. After
inspection, we came back and went to chow at
11:30.

How long does it take for my letters to get
to you?

Your brother,

Donald

Feb. 18, 1943

Dear Mom:

We really got a work out today. In the
morning we marched for three and a half hours,
and then we were almost dead. Lt. King looked
us over as we were drilling, and at first he said
we had a good company. But after watching us

a while longer, he "suggested" more drill. After chow, we went to small stores, so the men could get missing clothing. It was about four miles round trip. On the way up, the C.P.O. thought we were late, so he called double time at the bottom of a hill. About half the guys were dead ducks by the time we hit the top. After we got back, we went to physical fitness. That was the finisher. We first had a tug-o-war. After the first one, I couldn't even bend my fingers, and my fingers were plenty raw. We had two more, and they were plenty rugged. Then we had a rope climb. That's plenty tough. They must be trying to either make or break us. They're really stressing physical fitness. Every day about 3:30 until 4:20, we have a rugged session. They're going to get us in shape or else.

We had pie twice today, and the food has been swell lately. Inspector must have gone through. How are the chickens doing now? Have they picked up any? How about prices? I hear food is kind of hard to get. How are you doing?

Love, your son,

Donald

March 10, 1943

Dear Ellie:

Boy, are my feet sore tonight. We've been marching all day. This morning we went to colors at 7:35, and after that we had a physical fitness program for about an hour. I found out I had a lot of muscles I never knew I had before. After that we went to the barracks for a study period. Before chow we had rifle drill for about an hour. At 1:00, or 13:00 Navy time, we had drill with band. After the band left, we had more drill. Tonight a lot of the guys had holes in their shoes that they didn't have this morning.

Boy, am I glad I had my teeth fixed before I left. There was a man here that said he was called in to the dentist, and he had seven teeth filled in a row, without any Novocain. He said it almost killed him. I think I will have my tonsils out after I get out of Boot or as quick as I can.

We go on another week of work detail tomorrow. We work in ship service. After this work detail, we have a week left, and then we're through. After I graduate, I don't know where I'm going. Home I hope.

(Love,
Donald)

16

F-10 Marlinspike Instruction

Learning our knots

Mar. 23, 1943

Dear Pop:

A couple of companies of new boots in civilian clothes came in today and did they get a riding. The boys shot the breeze with them and told them every sort of story they could think up. They believed it too. I know I did.

I'm going to school...Motor Machinist school. We found out last night and were we happy. Most of the guys got what they wanted, but a few of them were griping though.

Today we were drilling with band and the regimental C.P.O. said we were undoubtably one of the best drilled companies ever to march in the drill hall. Tomorrow we go on liberty. I'm going to Spokane and see what it's like. We only get 12 hours though.

Oh no. I just found out that I don't go on liberty tomorrow. The dispensary claims I didn't have 2 of my shots, so I have to go over at 1300 to check up. The company leaves at 12:30, so I'll miss it. I'm going to have to wait until after graduation now for liberty.

Love, your son,
Donald

P.S. How is the food situation? Can you get enough?

Mar. 27, 1943

Dear Pop:

I'm out of boots! The company graduated yesterday in the drill hall, but I didn't get a chance to go, because I had a touch of Cat Fever. We got up at 4:00 this morning and transferred to O.G.U. (Outgoing Unit).

You should have seen the guys yesterday afternoon when they came back from graduation. They were the happiest guys I've ever seen. They threw their boots up in the air and gave out a loud hurrah. One thing I will say about not having boots is that it's cold on the legs!

Love, your son,
Donald

NAVY TRAINING SCHOOL

With boot camp behind them, many sailors went directly to sea. However, if a man needed special skills for the job he had been given, that sailor would go on to another training station. Many of these training schools were located on university campuses across the country. Others were located at navy training facilities such as Navy Pier in Chicago, Illinois.

Mar. 29, 1943

Dear Mom:

We're on our way. We left Farragut around 2:00 and have been moving perty slow. I can't tell you where I'm going, but I'll write as soon as I get there.

The train is all sailors, and we will be traveling for quite a while.

Love, your son,
Donald

4/1/43

Dear John:

We're here finally and is it heaven. We're going to the U. of Missouri. It's an 8 week course, and I have a good chance of coming out with a MoMM2 rating. We bunk six to a room and have lockers too. We have a 2 hour physical training period from 8 to 10 everyday, lecture from 10 to 12, and shop work from 1 to 5.

It's really a lot different place than Farragut.
Compared with Farragut, this place is heaven.
The chow that we had was really good, and I
guess we eat that good everyday. Also, all the
women...there are about 5 women to every man
here.

> Love, your brother,
> Donald

The University of Missouri

4-6-43

Dear Marg:

I finally got your letter, via Farragut, but it was in good shape even though it had been stamped all over. I thought your picture was most becoming.

We had our first navy period today, and we found out that we're in for a rugged conditioning period. It only lasts about an hour and a half, but oh, what our C.P.O. can do in that time!

We're still on elementary mathematics in shop, and it's getting awful boring. We're going to start tearing down the diesel engines perty soon, I hope. You ought to see some of the engines here. They're monsters.

Our graduation date has been set for our Company 16 for May 26th. I don't know what I'll get when I get out of here, but I should get more schooling before I go to sea. Right now a lot of them are getting P.T. boats, submarines, and invasion barges. If I get any of them, I hope I get submarine duty.

Love,

Donald

April 25, 1943

Dear Mom:

It's a lovely Easter here. This morning it rained and thundered for about an hour, so it is plenty wet out this morning. When I went to church, my pants got wet and were they ever itchy!!

I had a letter from Herbert dated the 19th and in it, it sounded like he wasn't going to get a leave to come home. I don't know. Maybe I'm wrong.

We've really learned a lot already. We've torn down a lot of engines and learned most of the parts. The fuel injector is about the most important part of a diesel and on them I'm perty sharp, so I think I'm in perty good shape so far.

We were paid this week, so you should have gotten my $20 allotment from the U.S. Navy too. If you haven't received it yet, it will most likely come soon. I signed up for a bond every three months which will be sent home. That doesn't go into effect until July however. That allotment really cuts into my pay. I received a rugged $14 today. I'm going to keep the money I have now until we graduate, so in case I get delayed orders, I will be able to come home.

We're wearing our white caps on liberty

now and our whites later on. I dread that day ,
because we're going to have a lot of washing!

Love, your son

Donald

May 26, 1943

Dear Pop:

I wish we had graduated today like you
thought, but we haven't. We don't get out until
Monday. We had our last test today, so now we
sit around until Monday. We will be able to
know whether we made our rating Saturday
when they give us our seating arrangement for
graduation. I think I've made my "Motor Mack".
I bought two white MoMM2/c rating badges
Saturday, which I hope to sew on soon.

The enclosed picture is a picture of the
guys in our room. On the left is Diemert. He's
from Montana and always is talking about how
good Montana is. The next guy is Tom Crow. He's
from Salt Lake City. The guy in the center is
Dave Spencer from Cleveland, Ohio. He is the
cut-up of our room. Whenever anything starts,
he is behind it. Last night we had a war until
about 11:00, and boy we really raised the roof.

That's me next, and the next guy is Joe Gusick.
He is from Minneapolis.

How are the chickens doing now? I suppose
the chicks are starting to get big now.

Love, your son,

Donald

June 11, 1943

Dear Mom:

Well, I made it to Chicago. I got here to
Navy Pier about 8:30 this morning. Is this place
ever big! There are several thousand sailors and
marines going to school here. We're in Company
18 and because we're rated men, we get liberty
every night. The classes and barracks are all in
the same building. The shop is downstairs, and
we're upstairs.

We've got a good deal except for the chow, and that isn't too bad. The diesel instruction is going to be the same as what we've had, so it's going to be plenty dry.

You should see the pigeons and squirrels here. They're so tame, that just as soon as we sit down on the bench at the park, they come right up to us. They must feed them a lot.

The U.S.O. is really swell here. There are ten floors, and they have almost everything. They give out free tickets to any place you want to go. I went to a show this afternoon on one of their tickets.

Love, your son,

Donald

Me at Buckingham Fountain in Chicago

June 30, 1943

Dear Marg:

We have a perty busy day here. At 6:00 the bugle gets us out of bed or is supposed to and then the guy on the public address system starts chanting: "It's 6:01, four minutes to go." We have to be up by 6:05 and have our mattress rolled back. He goes on until 6:05 and then says: "It's 6:05: MAA start taking names of men still in bed." If caught, it means a few hours extra duty. About 6:15 we're called for chow which generally isn't too good, and then at 7:15 we clean up our section. This week our section has an extra work detail, so I have to empty G.I.cans. We fall in for inspection at 7:45 every morning, and the chief or lieutenant sees that you're dressed properly. At 8:00 we're in lecture hall and from 9:45 to 10:45 we have a free period, which I am using now. At 10:45 we have physical until 11:35. It isn't so tough. It was worse at Missouri. We eat at about 11:40 and then report for shop at 12:45. Shop is the slowest period of the day. Four and a half hours of standing up. At 5:15 we march out of shop into the barracks, clean up, and go downtown. Life here at the Pier isn't so bad except for the chow.

This is a good town for anything you want to do. There are a lot of shows, ball games, places to swim, amusement parks, anything. We always have something to do. I went to a game between the Cubs and the Reds, but it was a perty dead game. The Cubs haven't much of a team this year. They have a park named Lincoln Park that is for service men, and it has everything. Tom Crow and I are going out there this afternoon.

Love, your brother,
Donald

July 28, 1943

Dear John:

Well, you can refer to me now as a radio star. Last night Spencer and I had a little chat on the radio over WGN.

Last Sunday I went out to the golf finals of the All American Open at Tam O'Shanter. I saw all the big shots: Byron Nelson, Sam Snead, Johnny Revolta, and a mess of others. Joe Louis played an exhibition round too. He is a perty good golfer too.

I'll be home on leave at 7:30. I hope somebody can be at the station to meet me.

Love,
Donald

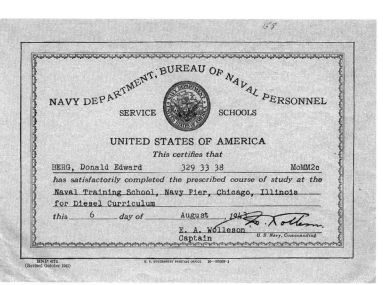

159

NAVY DEPARTMENT, BUREAU OF NAVAL PERSONNEL

SERVICE SCHOOLS

UNITED STATES OF AMERICA

This certifies that

BERG, Donald Edward   329 33 38   MoMM2c

has satisfactorily completed the prescribed course of study at the
Naval Training School, Navy Pier, Chicago, Illinois
for Diesel Curriculum

this 6 *day of* August , 1943

E. A. Wolleson
Captain   *U. S. Navy, Commanding.*

BNP 674
(Revised October 1942)   U. S. GOVERNMENT PRINTING OFFICE   16—05809-1

28

3
PREPARATION FOR SEA DUTY
THE COMMISSIONING OF THE PAKANA

With school completed and skills secured, sailors were assigned to various ships. There were the "big boys" like the aircraft carriers, battleships, and submarines. Smaller ships included the destroyers, the fast cruisers, and landing craft. The navy also had support vessels such as oil tankers, munitions ships, floating docks, and the workhorse of the navy, the tugboat. If the ship was already in full operation, the sailor boarded and took over his duties immediately. If, however, the ship was not yet commissioned for duty, the sailor would be assigned to a naval base where he would familiarize himself with the ship and help with preparations for sea duty.

The USS *Pakana* (ATF 108), a tugboat, was not yet completed and commissioned for duty when Donald Berg was assigned to the ship. He was stationed at Treasure Island, California, until the *Pakana* was commissioned on December 17, 1943.

The USS Pakana

Aug. 15, 1943

Dear Mom:

Well, we're here. We got in about 1 P.M. which is only a couple hours late, so that isn't too bad. We got into Oakland about 12:00, and then we rode the ferry across the bay to San Francisco for our first boat ride. The town looks kind of complicated and is built on a hill, so you go up and down hills in the middle of town.

We're going to look the town over this afternoon and then check in tonight at Treasure Island. I will send you my address as soon as possible.

Love, your son,

Donald

Oct. 11, 1943

Dear Marg:

From your report on dear old Park High, I would say that the team can't be so hot, although I might be wrong. How is the old place anyhow? Is there still life in the old place?

I received a letter from Dave Spencer today. He is out in the Atlantic on a "Tin Can" and doesn't know when he will be back. It took twenty days for his letter to get here.

You most likely noticed that I had a new address on my envelope. This morning I was transferred from the Annex to Treasure Island. I'm in a section with all the guys that are going to be on the Pakana. They seem to be a swell bunch of guys, and I think things are going to be O.K.

Love, your brother,
Donald

Oct. 12, 1943

Dear Pop:

Today we met the officers of the Pakana, and the results were good and bad. We have a swell warrant officer below deck, but the one on the topside is a perty rough character. He was telling us how things are going to be aboard the Pakana, and boy I'm telling you, he has everything strictly G.I. He really took us in hand too. He had an inspection. Told guys to get hair cuts and show up and in general gave everything a once over. He almost had my M.A.A. job taken away, but I talked fast enough so I could retain it.

The construction on the ship is about a month behind, so we won't be going out until about the last part of December. We're going to get fire fighting and gunnery next. We're going to learn how to handle the 20 mm's and the 3" so in case anything happens to the gunners, we can step in and keep on fighting.

The engineer warrant officer gave us a lecture on the ship, and the way he talks, it's going to be a sharp deal. He said we're even going to have depth charges on board which is something new.

Love,

Donald

October 18, 1943
Treasure Island
San Francisco, California

Dear John:

Today I received the first card since I left home after leave. It was the card about the game. Glad to hear that Park won 7 to 6.

In this letter I would like to explain to you a little of what we do here in a day. Well, in the first place, we get up about 7:00. Although we are supposed to get up a 5:30, we can't muster enough ambition to get up that early. When we do get up, it is time for chow, so we go over to the chow hall and get into the early chow line and go right in. If I didn't have my early chow pass, I would have to wait in a line that I believe is the slowest in the world. After chow, I come back to the barracks and sit around until I get a working party or some other detail. This morning I had to work in the pay line. I had to sit at a table and tell the men to fingerprint the back of their pay slip only with their five fingers. There is a place in front to stamp to, and they're always trying to fingerprint that too. Whenever they do, I have to say, "Sorry Doc, end of the line and make out a new pay slip." This burns them up, but they have been paid before, and they ought to know better by now. I was in that chair for three hours and then my pay number came along, and I got paid. I only got $25, and that is something I can't figure out. I should have had about $60, and I only got $25. I am going over to the pay office tomorrow and see if I can locate the rest of it. When I got out of the building, it was time for chow, so I went over and ate. They had perty good chow today too. They had beef steak, potatoes, gravy, good soup, pumpkin pie, and coffee, which I didn't drink. This afternoon I'm just laying around hoping that I won't get called for any work detail.

    The crew of the Pakana is beginning to assemble now, and they look like a good bunch of men. The only thing wrong with them is that they're almost all green. About 60% of them have never been to sea. This includes myself, naturally. I am a good U.S.N. man, and this 2/c Machinist behind me can't say that I am not, because I have an I.D. tag that says so. So there. That is to another M.A.A. who thinks I am a V6 sailor. The Chief B.M. of the Pakana is after the guys that work in the M.A.A. office again, and this time he is getting some of them. He hasn't contacted me as yet, and I am hoping that he won't

Can you send me the sports section from the papers? The only thing they have in the sports section here are racing forms and racing finals. I picked up most of the games last Saturday over the radio, but Minnesota wasn't on. They ought to be on this weekend, because they are playing Michigan and that is going to be one of the top team games of the nation. They even had a write up in one of the San Francisco papers, so it must be big. I hope I start getting some mail soon and hear about some of the things going on back in Minnesota.

Love,
Don

Dec. 7, 1943

Dear Pop:

You say I'm getting ready for sea duty? Well you aren't wrong. Right now we could pull out for the supply depot and take on supplies if we wanted to. They are all through except for cleaning up now, and from what I hear, they're going to run dock trials today.

All the members of the crew were allowed to invite friends for the commissioning on the 17th, so I hope to get an invitation card and send it home for a souvenir. We're supposed to go into commission at 10:00 and then leave for the supply depot at 12:30.

Don't worry if I don't write too often, because we have a lot of work to do the first few days after we're aboard ship.

Love,

Don

P.S. I got my Christmas present from Aunt Helen. She sent me a nice leather writing folder.

U. S. S. PAKANA
———
AUTHORIZED BY ACT OF
CONGRESS DECEMBER 17, 1941
KEEL LAID OCTOBER 1, 1942
LAUNCHED MARCH 3, 1943
SPONSOR: MISS LOUISE MARY SHIPP
COMMISSIONED DECEMBER 17, 1943

THE COMMANDING OFFICER
OFFICERS AND CREW OF THE U. S. S. PAKANA
REQUEST THE PLEASURE OF YOUR COMPANY
AT THE
COMMISSIONING CEREMONIES
TO BE HELD ON BOARD THE U. S. S. PAKANA
AT THE
UNITED ENGINEERING CO., LTD.
WEST ALAMEDA, CALIFORNIA

TIME: 10:00 a.m.
DATE: DECEMBER 17, 1943

Our crew at the Pakana's commissioning

December 19, 1943

Dear John:

Tonight I am on watch in the motor room, so I thought it would be a good time to drop you a line. So far everything has run smooth as silk. Friday morning we left T.I. and got to the ship about 9:30. After we had changed into our dress blues, we went up on the main deck for the commissioning ceremonies. After the captain had accepted the ship, we had our pictures taken, and I will try and get hold of one of them. We left United Engineers about 2:30 and went over to Oakland supply depot. I was in the steering room and everything went swell. After we had tied up, we started loading supplies immediately. We loaded until about 6:30, and then we knocked off for chow. The chow was the best I have tasted in a long time, and the main reason for that is that the cooks like to cook. They really put their hearts into it, and it comes out swell. Afterwards, I could have had liberty, but I didn't take it I was too tired to even move. I never thought you could get so tired running up and down ladders. We had taps at 10:00 and then had to get up at 6:00, and the time just flew. It seemed as though I just went to sleep. After breakfast we started loading again, and we loaded all day. Twice during the day we had a little excitement. About noon we heard a shot, and then we found out that the guard had fired the gun by mistake. Then later on another guard pulled the same stunt, so the warrant officer had them take the clips from the guns and put them in their belts. I guess he was afraid they would kill someone. Late last night we finished loading and if I do say so, I think we set a record for loading. We were here only 28 hours, and we're all loaded. We had a movie in the mess hall last night, and then we turned in. I had to get up at 3:30 for this watch, so I'm kind of sleepy now. Well, this brings me up to date for now.

Love,

Don

December 24, 1943

Dear Mom:

Well, I guess the letters from now on will be kind of incomplete. All the letters have to be censored, and we aren't to discuss the ship's movements or things of that sort. I'll write real often though and let you know I'm O.K.

Tonight I have the duty on the ship, but tomorrow I'm supposed to have liberty. I have hopes of getting out early and going to church if possible, but that all depends upon the skipper. He decides what time we get out.

I'm glad to hear John is doing so well trapping. I imagine the money is coming in handy.

Love,

Don

Dec. 27, 1943

Dear Marg:

Oh! but this is a salty crew. Yesterday we went outside of the bay into the ocean and about 30% of the crew got sea sick. I'm sorry to say that I have to include myself in that bunch too. Boy you don't know what kind of a feeling that is. One minute you're going straight down and the next minute you're going up. We were out there all day yesterday, and boy were we happy to go

39

under the "gate" and into the bay again. I just wonder how we will feel when we go out and stay out.

We had a good Christmas, although it could have been better. Christmas Day we got our presents from the Navy. We each got a gas mask, helmet, and life jacket. And they said, "Hang onto them." We had a good turkey dinner, and then they gave us liberty at 1:00, so we got ashore early.

In Pop's last letter were the clippings of the Park and Excelsior game. Please send me more. I like to know how Park is doing. Also if you want to, you can give me all the local dope, so that when I come home about eight months from now I won't be behind.

Love,

Don

P.S. Did you get my sea bag of gear?

My Christmas present from the Navy

4
SHORE DUTY

Not all sailors or soldiers during World War II saw overseas duty or battle. Many were stationed in the United States on shore duty or in other capacities. They were prepared to protect the United States in the event of an invasion. Many worked on repairing ships or vehicles damaged in the war. Others carried out a variety of jobs such as those related to ordering and delivery of supplies. Many servicemen prayed that they might stay in the United States, but others hoped to see some action in the war.

Jan. 12, 1944

Dear Mom:

This is the first time I have had to write in a long time, so I will try to make it a long one.

After we left San Francisco, we took a tow to San Pedro, and from there we went to San Diego. It took us about four days to get here, and when we first started out we had some fairly rough going. Anyhow I know I got sea sick, and I thought I was going to die. While I was sick, I wished I had never heard of the Navy. After awhile I got over it, and it wasn't too bad, although every time we go out in a little rough weather, I don't feel so good.

After we got here, we fooled around for a few days making test runs and such. This week-end we get our admiral's inspection, and then we're supposed to go back to San Francisco. Whether we do or not is something else.

Everything has been going all right. I'm

M.A.A. again in my section, and how I hate it. I have to wake everybody up in the morning, and they hate me for that, so I'm going to try and duck the job as soon as possible. The watches on the ship are simple, so we don't have any trouble there. The only thing wrong, though, is that we have to work all day and then stand watches at night. Since I came aboard, I've lost about seven pounds. Most of this was fat though, so I should get into perty good shape now.

I can see where I am going to save a lot of money being on this ship. I am enclosing a $65 money order, and I'll most likely send some more off and on later on. You should start to get my $50 allotment the 1st of February.

This is the end for now, and don't worry if I don't write too often, because sometimes it's kind of hard to get them mailed.

Love,
Don

Jan. 22, 1944

Dear Marg:

I guess it is about time I got another letter written. Time has been flying so fast that I haven't had time to write.

Yesterday we got into San Pedro, and we got 1:00 liberty. We went into Los Angeles first, and then we went to Hollywood. We saw the different movie and broadcasting studios, and then we went into a dance hall and saw Harry James. He is really all right. After that we fooled around and went back to the ship. We're supposed to go out tomorrow, and I'm not sure where we are going.

We had our inspection, and it went over O.K. They have let up on us a little now, so things are fairly good now. The only thing is that we don't get enough sleep. I guess I'll have to get along on less.

I got my candy from Helen.

Love,

Don

Jan. 30, 1944

Dear Marg:

Seems as though you have become a regular wolf since I left. By your letters, you seem to be doing all right with the boys. I hope I'm not embarrassing you, Marg, by saying this.

We're at United Engineers for repairs now, and I guess we will be here for awhile. We're supposed to get coast duty, so I'm hoping.

The weather here isn't too bad. It rains quite a bit, and it is kind of cold, but otherwise it's O.K.

The other day I did something I shouldn't have done, so now I am restricted for two weeks.

I hope I don't go nutty before I get out.

We've got our pictures of the crew now, and I'll try and send them tomorrow if I can.

Marg, I guess I didn't mention this before, but I want to tell you that I'm mighty lucky to be in the states now. If we hadn't had a change of orders, we would almost be in Pearl Harbor by now. When we were in San Pedro, we were supposed to take two oil barges to Pearl Harbor. They were connected up, and we were all ready to sail when a change in orders came through. I can say we were mighty lucky. I hope we don't come that close again for quite awhile.

Have you got any more pictures I haven't seen? I could go for some more photographs. They buck up my morale about as much as anything when it is low. Thanks!

Love,

Don

Some of our crew. That's me second from the right.

March 6, 1944

Dear Pop:

Well, it looks like the time has come when we're to go across. Tomorrow we are supposed to leave for Pearl Harbor in a convoy with other tugs. After we get there, we might come back to the States and we might not.

We are in San Pedro now, and we've been here a couple days. Last night we had liberty, so we went to Hollywood. We fooled around there until about 10:20, and then we started back. It's about 30 miles from Hollywood to Pedro by car, so we decided to hitchhike. We got about 10 different rides, and finally got back around 2:30, so we made perty good time. Last night's liberty was most likely to be my last liberty in the U.S. From now on, it will be Honolulu for liberty. I've talked to guys that have been there, and they say it is perty nice. The only thing wrong is that you have to be in before sunset, so we won't be going out nights.

The weather here is swell. The other day when we were coming in, we didn't have anything to do, so we thought we would get a sun tan. We got a tan all right and then some. Some of the guys really got burned. Yesterday was a swell day, and it was really swell to be out in the sun.

Oh yes! Last night when we walked past the C.B.S. in Hollywood, we noticed a lot of

45

women around, and I said, "I bet Frank Sinatra is going to be on tonight." Sure enough, he was. We tried to get in, but we couldn't.

Well, this ends the Navy news and if we do go over, I'll write as soon as we get there.

Love, your son,

Donald

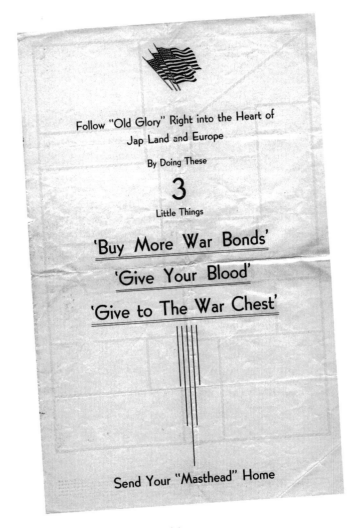

Follow "Old Glory" Right into the Heart of
Jap Land and Europe

By Doing These

3

Little Things

'Buy More War Bonds'

'Give Your Blood'

'Give to The War Chest'

Send Your "Masthead" Home

5
OUT TO SEA

U.S. Navy sailors may have been stationed on ships in the Atlantic or the Pacific. Those headed toward the action in the Pacific often stopped first at Pearl Harbor, the main base for that area. Before the invasion of Pearl Harbor on December 7, 1941, sailors never dreamed that this base could be hit by Japanese bombers. However, after the invasion, all ships were on alert as soon as they left U.S. shores.

Censorship of letters occurred on each individual ship. Sailors were not allowed to write about their locations, their missions, or their adventures. If they did, the ship censor would cut or mark out that portion of the letter.

During this time at sea, the USS *Pakana* conducted salvage operations, repairs or refloating of craft, and towing operations at Pearl Harbor, the Marshall Islands, Kwajalein Atoll, Guam, and the Palau Islands.

March 27, 1944

Dear Pop:

I finally got some mail, but it wasn't too fresh. Most of it was perty old, but then I'm hoping for a new batch soon.

I've been feeling perty good lately, and as a matter of fact, I've felt perty good ever since I came aboard. I've gained back my weight, and I guess I weigh about 173 lbs. now which is good enough for me.

I'm going to get off my Master at Arms Job at the end of this month, I hope. I really hate to go around and wake the guys up in the morning. When I wake them up, they groan and ask what time it is. When I tell them, they groan again and try to go back to sleep, but I see to it that they don't. After I get them up, I'm all worn out, because it really is a battle on some of them. The other duties of the job aren't too bad, but I'll still be glad to get relieved by someone else.

Mar. 30

Sorry about this letter. I kind of slacked off for a couple days, because there wasn't much to say.

We're getting paid soon, I guess. I'm drawing about sixty dollars, and at the rate I'm spending my money here, well I think it will last for a long time. It is perty hard to spend too much money.

I had a letter from Dave Spencer today, and I guess he is still on the east coast. Anyhow, he still raves about New York. Well, this has to do, because I can't think of anything more to say.

Love, your son,

Donald Edward Berg

April 12, 1944

Dear John:

Boy, this is really a job to write letters. Everything that I would like to write about would be cut out, so I guess I'll just have to think of all the unmilitary things we do.

Awhile ago our mascot was killed, so tonight we thought it was time we got another. We got a little white and brown pup that is really cute. She has kind of a dumb look on her face, but then I guess she doesn't have to be a "whiz kid" to get along on here.

I imagine that by the time you get this letter, Herbert will be home on leave. I hope he makes the best of it, because once he gets out of the U.S.A., he won't get another for quite awhile. I know that I don't expect any for quite awhile.

I've made a couple liberties here, but they didn't amount to much. Most of it is just going ashore and then coming back. Well, I've over done myself now.

Love, your brother,
Donald Edward Berg

Our mascot

49

June 26, 1944

Dear Pop:

Received your letter today and was very glad to receive it. I'm still about the same.

Ellie's ducks are surely getting big. Mom said they weighed about 3 1/2 lbs. They must have put on weight fast. Tell Ellie to fry one up and send it out (just kidding, Ellie!).

We get perty good stuff on the radio. We get news, music, and other programs. Sometimes we get Radio Tokyo, and boy, that is fun to listen to. According to them, we have lost the war and are foolish to keep on fighting. That's the way they figure, but we have different ideas.

John and Marg ought to take advantage of the chance to make some money. When John gets his car, I suppose he will think he is really up in the world. Just tell him to take it easy and not for him to think he is the king of the road. Just a little advice from his bigger brother.

Well, I guess I'll knock off as I have the watch in the morning.

Love,

Don

July 1, 1944

Dear Mom:

Well, today is John and Marg's birthday. I
hope they got my birthday present. I think I sent
it in plenty of time.

I'm fine, and the conditions aren't too bad
here. We get swim call quite a bit, and boy, the
water is swell. We dive off the side of the ship.
The water is nice and clear and just the right
temperature. When you get salt down your
throat though, it isn't so good. Anyhow, it is a lot
of fun and a good form of relaxation.

I'm sorry to say it, but you are wrong. I
haven't been close to the states for quite awhile.
The reason for that fast letter was that it most
likely made perfect plane connections. I sometimes get letters like that too, and then other
times I get some that are a month or a month and
a half old. Even so, any mail is welcome. Write
soon, because mail is scarce.

Love,

Don

Liberty in Honolulu

At the beach in Honolulu.
That's me on the right.

Me, on top of the pyramid!

Liberty in Honolulu. I'm on the left.

Aug. 29, 1944

Dear Ellie:

 I imagine that by the time you get this
letter, you, Marg, and John will have started
school again. I know that you will most likely
hate to go back, but as for myself, I know that I
would like to go back right now. Sometimes when
I sit down and think of all the fun I had in high
school, I wish very much that I were back there.
Right now, I have serious thoughts of going to the
U. of Minnesota when I get out. In that way, I
figure I'll get in a little schooling and then sort
of a vacation all at once.

 Lately I have been sleeping in my hammock
on topside, so I can get some fresh air. The fresh
air is swell, but every now and then I fall out or
the line breaks. Any way you look at it, I hit the
deck and it isn't soft. I'll learn one of these days
though.

You know, Ellie, you ought to have a lot of money by the time I get back. At the rate you are making it, you ought to have the old sock full in no time. I think it would be a good idea to hang onto some of that cabbage.

Has John bought his car yet? If he has, I hope he got a good deal. Have him write and tell me about it.

Love,

Don

P.S. Have you any more pictures you can send me?

6
TOUGH TIMES

Sailors and soldiers had similar fears and feelings. When feelings of homesickness or worry about others in the war didn't get to them, the real fear of death always lingered.

Sept. 15, 1944

Dear Pop:

Well, here is one of my few letters to you. You don't know how hard it is to write about something. The things that are worth writing about are censored, and then what's left isn't worth writing about.

Last time we got mail, I got a card from Herbert with an overseas address from New York. Has he left yet? If he has, I don't suppose he will see any action, because from the news reports, it won't last much longer over there. From all reports, those boys are really going to town. I hope we start moving out here, that way too, so we can all go back home.

The other day I was reading in an old paper that we had aboard that the U.S.S. Tide had been sunk. Dave Spencer was on her, and then there were some other guys I knew too. I surely hope they got off all right. I had planned to go down to Cleveland and see Dave when I got back.

I'm enclosing a money order for $40.

Love,

Donald E. Berg

Sept. 20, 1944

Dear Marg:

How do you like to be back in school again? I imagine you're all in the heat of things, what with football starting and all the other things that go with it. Right now I wish I had my high school days to do over again. I know that I would take advantage of a lot of things I passed up.

Today we really had a treat. We had ice cream for the first time in about three or four months and Marg, it really tasted good! You don't come to realize how much you like a thing until after you miss it for awhile, and boy, I really like my ice cream.

I'm still all right and feeling fine with the exception of that heat rash. It is about enough to drive you nuts after you start to sweat awhile. About the only cure for it is time, so I guess I'll have to weather it out.

We are seeing country but most of the time it is water. Out here most of the islands are about the same. Flat and covered with coconut trees. I suppose you are still wondering where I'm at. - Well, it doesn't make too much difference. One place is as good as another out here. If you're still too inquisitive, take out a world atlas map of the Pacific and start guessing. You might guess it! I've been a lot of places.

Have you gotten any word from Herbert in Europe yet?

Love,

Don

November 1, 1944

Dear John:

I received a lot of letters yesterday, and now I'll try and answer yours at least. I had a letter from Herbert the other day, and he seems to be all right.

The other day I received a letter I never wanted to get. It was from Dave Spencer's dad, and he said Spence had been killed when his ship went down. The other kid I knew on there from Minneapolis was hit, but he got off all right. Boy, Spence was a guy I really wanted to see come through, because we made some good liberties together, and I was going to Cleveland to see him after the war. That is out now. Makes you think.

Things are fine for me as usual, and now we are going to have a chance to make a liberty. It has been better than five months since we had our last liberty, and I guess you know that I am going to take advantage of the one we get. I've got the money, and I'm not afraid to spend it.

I hope you made out all right in the class play. I would surely like to have seen it. Boy, I can just see you up on the stage. I hope you didn't get stage fright!

Love, your brother,

Don

Bay Village Oct. 2

Dear Mr. Berg — We received the letter you wrote to David. I don't just know how to answer it but David was killed when his ship was sunk June 7 we had a letter from his Lt Commander saying that the ship was sunk from an under water explosion it seems there were only a few survivors. the last letter we had from David was dated May 17. it seems every where we look around here is his things that he loved so well and enjoyed so much that he will never see again but have to make th

November 24, 1944

Dear Mom:

I received your last letter in four days
which is really O.K. Most of them have been
taking 6 or 7 days, but this one really came
straight through in record time.

The other day on liberty I went to a picture studio and had some pictures taken. I got
some five x seven's and when I get them, I'll send
them rushed to you.

How did John make out in the class play?
I hope he did all right.

Yes, we have had a chance to get bananas
and pineapples. The other day I had a banana
split that was really swell.

We have a little kitten aboard now, and it
reminds me of Billy exactly. They are just about
the same only the kitten on here isn't afraid of
anybody. Even the dog doesn't bother it.

I had a letter from Herbert yesterday, and
he seems to be getting along all right. I just hope
he doesn't get caught like that again. That was
too close for comfort! It would seem that he did
see quite a lot of action before he got hit.

I guess that about does it.

Love, your son,

Don

P.S. Mom, I'm enclosing a money order for

thirty dollars for you to buy John, Marg, Ellie, Pop, Aunt Helen, and yourself a Christmas present. I would have bought them here, but there is so much red tape to mail them. I want you to get them something nice and sign the cards for me.

Don

December 19, 1944

Dear Ellie:

Here it is only six days before Christmas. It surely seems funny with no snow or anything...doesn't seem like Christmas at all. I just hope I don't have to miss next Christmas. Two is enough for me, I hope.

I'm really glad to hear Herbert is getting better. He must have been hit perty hard to have taken this long to be able to sit up.

I guess that about does it, but in closing I want to wish everyone a very Merry Christmas, and I hope I'll be able to get home for the next one.

Love,
Don

Herbert

December 24, 1944

Dear John:

Boy, the old European war isn't going any to well these days, is it? I Just hope Herbert wasn't too close to the German lines when the breakthrough came.

On board ship here, we have a couple musicians, Last night they were playing Christmas songs which really made me blue, It doesn't seem much like Christmas here, but when I start thinking about what it is like back home right now, I really wish I was there. Well, anyhow, maybe I can make the next one. I hope I will, but then again maybe I won't. I guess I'll get home eventually,

That does it for tonight.

Love,

Don

December 26, 1944

Dear Mom:

Boy, how the time flies. It doesn't hardly seem possible that I have been in the Navy for two years. I don't know where the months have gone to, but they have really flown by. A lot of guys on here feel sorry for themselves, because they have to be in the Navy, but I don't regret it a bit. In the past two years, I have learned an awful lot that I know I would never have learned if I had been a civilian all this time. No sir, I don't regret it a bit. Of course, it is a little tough at times being away from home, but I guess I can get by.

Yesterday was one of those tough days, but it didn't turn out too bad. We had holiday routine all day and a swell Christmas dinner which was O.K. I had a chance to go to church in the morning. When we sang all those Christmas carols, I got kind of homesick. But other than that, it was really nice. I just hope Herbert and I can get home for next Christmas and don't have to miss anymore for awhile.

Awhile ago John wrote and said he was going to join up when school was out. I surely hope he doesn't do that. He would be a lot smarter to finish out school and get his diploma. He might not think it is worth much now, but he will find out later that it means a lot. After the war a man is going to need an education to get ahead, because there are going to be an awful lot of smart guys to compete with.

I'm going to start and put in a correspondence course on heating and ventilation. After that, I want to put one in on air conditioning and refrigeration. They are courses I know I can use after the war, and I know I'll have plenty of time to put them in now. I want to be a Jack of all trades, so I'll be able to get along. I don't want to end up digging ditches, if I can do something else a lot better.

Well, all for now. Happy New Year!

Love, your son,

Don

Feb. 13, 1945
At Sea

Dear Pop:

Well, we're out here riding the old waves again, and it isn't bad. I hope I can get a little state side shore duty in a few months. Shore duty and I get along just fine.

I've been sleeping topside the last couple of nights and boy, it really gets cool. Reminds me of the times when we used to camp out back home.

Hey, you ought to see the mustache I'm trying to grow. It hasn't a bad start, and in a couple three months I ought to have something. That is if I can stand it that long.

In case I don't get another letter off before Mom's birthday, I want to wish her a very happy birthday, and I hope we can all be home for her next one.

I heard from Herbert yesterday, and he says he is in fine shape again. He finally got my letters too. He has been wondering for a long time why I hadn't written.

On board ship we have quite a few musicians, and they really turn out some good music. They kind of make you homesick at times though when they play songs that were popular when we were there.

Have you any more pictures developed? They are something I really like to receive in a letter. All for tonight.

Love, your son,

Don

7
TYPHOON

The United States fleet in the Pacific was not only battered by the Imperial Japanese Navy. Several times during World War II, nature struck a blow to U.S. ships. Western Pacific typhoons are the most powerful storms on the planet, and many of them can generate winds in excess of 130 knots (about 150 mph).

The most destructive typhoon during the war occurred on December 18, 1944. It sank three American destroyers, and seven other ships were badly damaged. Admiral Chester W. Nimitz, the commander in chief of the Pacific Fleet, reported that losses in lives were great: nearly 800 sailors were killed by the storm.

In June 1945, another huge typhoon struck unsuspecting ships. The greatest damage was sustained by the cruiser *Pittsburgh* when her 104-foot bow broke completely off the ship. The *Pakana* endured several of these storms and was the tug, in conjunction with the USS *Munsee* (ATF 107), that salvaged the bow of the Pittsburgh.

SHIPS ENCOUNTER HEAVY WEATHER OFF OKINAWA.

U S NAVY PHOTO 126-18

March 18, 1945

Dear John:

Received quite a few letters and basket-
ball scores yesterday. Glad to hear that Park is
still in the district meet.

That Navy air crew deal ought to be O.K.,
but you don't want to figure on it too much. I
know a lot of guys that got in and had everything planned, and then something came up that
changed everything. You will probably get it all
right, but don't get discouraged if they put you
in something else.

Well, we finally got a break. The Navy
censor has eased up on regulations, so we can
write about the places we have been and the
things we have done. From Pearl, I went south to
the Marshall's and had quite a bit of duty at
Eniwetok. While there, I really saw a battle fleet.
When they are all lined up, it is really something
to see. From Eniwetok, I went to Guam and saw
part of the action there. The island itself is
really perty, but it didn't smell too good then.
There were an awful lot of dead marines and
Japs on the beach and in the water. I didn't see
any planes in the air, but there were a couple
Jap planes on the beach that had been shot
down. Some of the guys got souvenirs, but I
didn't get any.

A few weeks later I had about the most

66

exciting moments of my life. That was riding out
a typhoon. The ship was bouncing around like a
cork, and there were a couple of sharks following
us that must have thought they had chow on the
way. We weathered it though, and I later went
back to Pearl. Stayed there quite awhile and
got in quite a bit of liberty. Played golf and got
a lot of good swimming in, but good things don't
last forever. Now I'm headed central Pacific
way again. I don't know how long I'll be down
here this time, but I hope I'll be going back to the
states when we head east again.

　　　Well, all for now.

　　　　　　　　Your brother,

　　　　　　　　　　Don

Horseback riding on Diamond Head, Hawaii

Liberty in Honolulu (that's me on the bottom right).

8
TIME OF CRISIS

There were many large battles for control of islands in the Pacific. From the American loss at Bataan, the Philippines, in February of 1942 to the battles of Kwajalien, Eniwetok, Saipan, Guam, and Iwo Jima, U.S. soldiers, marines, and sailors risked their lives in their bid to stop Japan from their control of the Pacific. No battle, however, was quite as fierce as the Battle of Okinawa, which began in April of 1945. The Fifth U.S. Navy Fleet endured 1,500 Japanese kamikaze attacks. These were suicide bombers who would not hesitate to crash their planes into American ships when all else failed. The Japanese did not give up the fight for Okinawa until June of 1945. It was the last major battle of the war, and when it was finished, American casualties totaled 39,000 with over 12,000 dead or missing.

The USS *Pakana* was assigned as a member of a screen for a task unit which left on March 25th to sail for Nansei Shoto, Okinawa Shima. During this time, the *Pakana* opened fire on enemy aircraft that attacked the unit, assisted landing craft in retracting from the beach on Okinawa, and picked up survivors from ships that had been hit or sunk by the kamikaze attacks. On April 6, 1945, the *Pakana* rescued 34 enlisted men and officers of the USS *Bush* (DD 529) from the water. Many of the crew gave artificial respiration and medical aid as directed by the Pharmacist Mate.

On April 16th, the *Pakana* was dispatched to tow the USS *Laffey* (DD 724). The *Laffey* had been hit by 22 Japanese suicide aircraft off Okinawa and had survived the damage. It was later known as the ship that wouldn't die.

The *Pakana* survived a kamikaze attack on the morning of May 28th. Coxswain Paul A. Wing, of Rochester, Vermont, was on lookout watch. He ran to the nearest 20mm gun and in a few moments he sent the suicide plane crashing into the sea less than 100 yards from the ship. He was awarded the Silver Star and presented with a $1,000 war bond by his thankful shipmates.

ROCKETS SOFTEN OKINAWA BEACH.   U S NAVY PHOTO 126

BATTLESHIP ROARS SUPPORT OF OKINAWA INVADERS. 1 APRIL, 1945. U S NAVY PHOTO. 126-10

April 26, 1945

Dear Mom:

Some more back mail caught up with us yesterday, and I got the Easter card and large envelope with the church newspaper and the Reader's Digest. The pictures were really good too. Then too, I received my course in heating and air conditioning from the Armed Forces Institute. It is a course similar to a correspondence course, and it looks like it will be really all right.

Things are about the same as usual, although at times my blood pressure really takes a beating!!

The war in Germany is really going all

right, isn't it? Boy, I hope they get it over with there and start to work on this side. Herbert ought to have a perty good chance to get back home too after they're through, and then maybe I'll get a chance to see him out here. Well, my mind has turned a complete blank, so all for now.

Love, your son,

Don

May 11, 1945

Dear John:

Well, I guess if I am coming home on or before May 15, I will have to hurry. At the rate transfers have been coming in, I'm afraid you are going to be off the mark about six months, and maybe then I'll make it if I'm lucky. I surely hope I can make it home for Christmas though.

So you are perty rusty with the old "hooks." Well, you know what they say, "Practice makes perfect." Boy, I surely wish I was back there getting a little practice in with the old golf clubs.

The other day we got the word about the German surrender over the radio, and were we happy! Boy, we would have all gone out and had a party if there was any place to go. But there wasn't, so we just stayed aboard and hoped that this one will be over soon too.

Most of the guys got kind of mad at the

dope that is coming in over the radio now. The way it sounds, you would think the war was all over and everybody can knock off. But let me tell you, we still have a tough fight ahead. The Japanese are tough and crazy in the way they fight, and that makes things all the tougher. I think if they brought some of the civilians out from the states to see what was going on, they would soon change their minds.

Well, enough lecturing for now. Drop me a few more lines soon.

Your brother,

Don

May 29, 1945

Dear Mom:

Well, here it is the 29th. I suppose John, Marg, and Ellie will be getting out of school today, and they will be mighty happy to be out. Well, as for me, I wish I were back there and could go to school and only had teachers to think about.

Awhile ago I wrote Bea of the Beacon in the newspaper and told her that a prayer was all that was needed at times out here. Well, I want to say to whoever has been praying for us that his prayers have been answered. I could go into details, but I don't think the censor would allow it.

I received a box of candy from Helen the other day, and it really tasted good. It made perty good time getting here, so it was still fresh.

I heard over the radio that the first army is on its way back to the states, and I'm really glad to hear that. You ought to be seeing Herbert soon. Give him my regards, and tell him to take the town apart for me once, and I'll do the same for him when the time comes for me to see good old Minneapolis again.

All for now.

Love, your son,

Don

June 1, 1945

Dear Pop:

Again I take my pen in hand, as the old folks used to say, to let you know that everything is all right.

I'm enclosing a money order for $100 to sock away in the bank. Some day in the future I may need it. I've been thinking a lot on post war ideas, but I haven't decided on anything certain yet. More than one night I've lain in my sack, not being able to sleep and just thinking. I've thought of a lot of ideas, but I don't know if they would work out or not. Time will tell, I guess.

     We have had some perty good movies lately. Most of the guys' nerves are perty high strung right now, including myself, and it does us all a lot of good to get something to laugh at, and boy, I guess you know we do! If we ever went to a regular movie house, we would all be thrown out. Most of the time, we have a movie in the afternoon, so that is O.K. We used to have them at night, but we found out that wasn't very wise. All for now.

         Love, your son,
            Don

STARS AND STRIPES RAISED ON OKINAWA.

U.S. NAVY PHOTO 128-6

July 4, 1945

Dear Marg:

Here it is the 4th of July again. Boy, the years surely do roll around fast. A year ago today I was on a beach in the Marshalls, and two years ago I was in Navy pier in Chicago. I surely hope I'll be able to spend my next 4th of July at home seeing the fireworks at Powderhorn Park!

I'm really glad to hear that Pop gave some blood. I know he should not have done it, but someday there might be somebody out here that will be mighty glad he did it.

From what I have been able to gather, I imagine you will be seeing Herbert soon. I surely wish I could get back too, and we could make it an old home week, but I guess it will be like it has been in the past. First he gets home, and then I come trailing in after he has gone.

I'm still fine, and from the way things stand now, I don't think there will be any change. If at times the mail from me is rather thin, don't worry, because there is usually a good reason, Although at times, I get in a rut and can't seem to write at all.

All for now.

Love, your brother,

Don

July 6, 1945

Dear Ellie:

This time I'm going to make sure that you don't have to write two letters in a row without an answer from me.

The other day we were told by the censor board that some of our travels could be related and here goes.

After I left Pearl, I went to Ulethli and from there to my first major invasion. Things were quiet all the way up, and we were beginning to wonder just how bad this was going to be. Well, when the ship I was attached to and the rest of them pulled into Okinawa, things were still quiet. A beachhead was established without loss, and the Jap inactivity really had us thinking. A few days later, the Japs began to show themselves. Fighting became hard on the beach, and the Jap air force was coming out strong. One night we were called to go out and assist a ship, the Bush, that had been hit, but before we got there, it sank. We had to pick up survivors. We found a bunch of them on a floater net, and some of them were perty far gone. I got one of them that had nearly drown and had to give him artificial respiration. All the time another fellow and I were working on him, I was wishing I had learned how better in school, because now I was afraid that if I didn't do it right, I might kill him. After

The USS Bush

a couple hours, he pulled out of it and felt perty good, but he was still perty badly shocked. Going back we had G.Q., and boy I was hoping and praying nothing would happen then with the extra men aboard. Well, we got in all right, and the next morning we put them on a different ship. When they left, they couldn't say "thanks" enough.

A few nights later, we were out and a Jap torpedo plane came in on us. His fish missed, and we knocked him down as he went away. I guess you know we were mighty glad to get into port a few hours later. Things were never quiet after the first few days of the invasion. Jap planes were in the air all the time. One afternoon we went out to help another ship in, and that is where I met Dick Lovelett. He came aboard when we got in, so we sat around and talked for a couple of hours. Boy, it really feels good to meet someone you used to know in civilian life.

Later on, we got another call to go and get a burning ship. Coming back, a Jap Betty came over, and he didn't have a chance. The old gunners got their guns on him and down he went. Well, we figured that would end our Jap hunting for the day, but it didn't. We got in around 7:00 in the morning, Just in time to see some "tin cans" shoot down a Jap bomber. We were afraid he was going to get away, but then they got him. He exploded Just like a skyrocket on the 4th of July, and all there was left was small pieces of the plane coming down. About 2 hours later, a Jap kamakazi came out of the clouds and right down towards us. He was strafing, and boy, you should have seen us dive for cover. One man was on one of the guns, and he was really pouring the lead into him. About 100 yds. away, he exploded and hit the water. Ellie, I'm telling you, my knees were shaking for an hour afterwards. A couple weeks later, we pulled out of there to go to a rest area.

Well, that is all for now, and I'll write again soon.

Love,

Don

P.S. That puzzle has Just about driven me nuts. One guy has gotten it, so far, and the rest of them are still banging their heads on the wall!

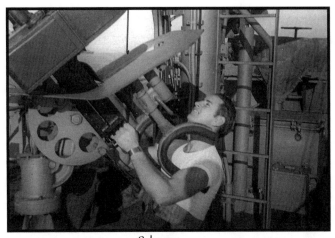

Pakana gunner

July 30, 1945

Dear Mom:

Received your letter saying that Herbert was home. Boy, I guess you know that kind of makes me homesick to hear that. At times I get to feeling I'm never going to get back, but I guess I'll make it in due time. The Navy has come out with a new deal now too. After 24 months overseas, we're eligible to go back to the states for a 30 day leave and then report back to the ship, so I should make it home before the war is over. I hope! I've been thinking a lot on post war stuff lately, and I've figured it out that a chicken farm would be my best bet. I think that a fairly good-sized farm could make good money if it was run right. Right now I have a lot of ideas on it that I think would work out.

I'm still fine and dandy. Had a cholera

79

JAP PLANE DIVING ON U. S. CARRIER. GOOD GUNNERY
GOT HIM IN TIME.

U S NAVY PHOTO 107-12

shot the other day that kind of gave my arm a bad time, but it is all right now. They never used to bother me much before, but I guess the heat has something to do with it here.

The war news has really been good lately, hasn't it? The air force has the Japs on the run now, and I imagine they will keep them going.

We used to listen to Radio Tokyo a lot of the time, and we had to laugh. The way they talk, they have just about won the war. Lately they have begun to say that they will fight for twenty years, if necessary, and that they will never give up, but I think they will change their tune soon.

I'm enclosing some Jap invasion money that

they used in the Philippines. It's worthless, so
don't try and spend it. Ha!

Well, all for now.

Love, your son,

Don

P.S. Tell Herbert to look up the 108 if he
gets out here, and I will welcome him aboard at
the gangway!!

Aug. 2, 1945

Dear Pop:

Received your July 22 letter yesterday.
Surely made good time getting here.

I'm still fine and dandy and waiting for
the day when I'll get some state-side orders like
Herbert did.

You remember how I never did like coffee?
Well, I still don't. Most of the guys like their
coffee perty strong, and that doesn't agree with
me. When I do drink it, I have to fix it up a lot.
If you drink it straight, you have to be set for a
jolt. Man, that stuff could take the lining off
your stomach without half trying, and I mean it
is that strong. Right now, I could go for a nice
cold glass of milk, but of course you can't get
any out here. Every time I've gotten back to
Pearl, I've always caught up on milk and ice

cream, but good. They are two things I can't get enough of.

You're right about a lot of guys being nervous wrecks after doing a lot of fighting. When I met Dick Lovelett at Okinawa, he was about that way himself. His ship had been hit, but he wasn't even scratched and then that night when we were tied up to them, a stray bullet grazed off his head. Boy, after that he was shaky until he left. Surely am glad he made it back to the states all right.

We had a place up there we called Grave-yard Gulch, because that was where most of the ships were being hit. Boy, I (and I think everybody else) just hated to go up there, and that is one place I don't want to ever see again. Another thing that we didn't go for was the moon. Back in the states a full moon is swell, but out there we would have liked more than once to have shot it out of the sky. When it came up, it was just like a huge spotlight had come on, and don't think the Japs didn't know how to use it, because I know for sure they did.

Well, enough of this stuff for now. I want Herbert to send me his address as soon as he gets to California, so that if I get back within the next 2 or 3 months, I want to try and see him.

Love, your son,

Don

9
V-J DAY

At 7:00 p.m. on August 14, 1945, President Truman announced that the Japanese had surrendered. This surrender took place after the United States dropped atomic bombs on Hiroshima and Nagasaki, Japan, on August 6th and 9th respectively. It would not be until September 2, 1945, on the USS *Missouri* anchored in Tokyo Bay that the Allied powers and Japan would sign the surrender agreement. On the night of the surrender, men of the *Pakana* hoisted mops and brooms up the mast to signify a "clean sweep" as part of their celebration.

August 15, 1945

Dear Marg:

Well, the war is over, and I guess everyone is happy except maybe the Japanese. But then I guess they are happy it is over too. When we got the news today, everybody went wild. It was only our fourth celebration, but it was still the best. Everyone knocked off work and started talking about when we were going to get back to the "states", that place I've been away from way too long. I figure it will take quite some time before the Navy will release large numbers of men, but most of the guys can see themselves home already. Getting out is one thing I don't have to worry about yet. My enlistment isn't up until Jan. 46, so I've six months to wait before I can even think about getting out. That doesn't worry me though, because I'm happy enough now that the war is over and that we can start thinking of peace time living again. Boy, that's for me!

Well all for now, and I'll be home in six months, I hope.

Love,

Don

P.S. Didn't get to mail this last night. So much excitement going on. Every time we get a new report on the surrender, everybody goes wild. Last night they were shooting up skyrockets and

blowing horns for about an hour when we got
some more dope. Surely hope they get all the
details settled soon, or we will go nuts just waiting. All now.

      Don

                         Sept. 2, 1945

Dear Pop:

   Today we heard the formal surrender of
Japan over the radio from a radio ship in Tokyo
Bay. Boy, that really sounded good too. I only
wish I could have been there.

   Some admiral was talking too about the
navy discharge plan. He really made things
sound good too. By his talk, I figure I should get
out by next spring, and that would be really all
right.

   Received Mom's Aug. 16 letter today, and
from what you said, I can imagine that there was
quite a hot time in Minneapolis when they announced the surrender. Boy, I would like to have
been there.

   I received the box of candy Mom sent, and
it was in perty good shape. I got Mrs. Smith's box
too on the same day. Both boxes of Fanny

Farmer were really all right.

Have any of the guys around home been discharged yet? I was just thinking that if I got home on leave, there wouldn't be anybody to go out with except women... but then I guess that wouldn't be so bad.

Well, all for now, and I'll be home in a few months, I hope.

Love, your son,

Don

10
NAGASAKI

On September 29, 1945, the USS *Pakana* was ordered to report to the Port Director at Nagasaki, Japan. So little was known about the atomic bomb that when the sailors of the *Pakana* entered the harbor at Nagasaki, they were amazed by the destruction. The *Pakana* acted as a harbor tug in that area until October 16th, when it left for Okinawa.

Sept. 25, 1945

Dear Pop:

Two days ago we got our first look at Japan. We are now in Kago Shima Bay waiting for orders.

When we got to Okinawa, we stayed there for two days and then came right up here. The trip up was swell. No Japs or anything. Coming in here we went through a long channel, and there were a lot of Japanese villages along the banks. Everything was so peaceful that you could hardly think we had fought a war with them. The reason we were sent here was to pull two ships off the beach, but they were up so far, I doubt if we can get them off. There are only three ships in here besides us, and two of them are on the beach. There was a typhoon in here a little while ago that put them there, and boy, it flattened a lot of Japanese houses too. About half of them along the beach where we are anchored are squashed too.

All day the first day in, we watched them through high powered glasses, and there wasn't too much to see. There were a lot of Jap soldiers on the beach, but they were unarmed. They really work their women too. All day they did the heavy work, and using the crudest methods too. I haven't seen anything modern yet. Behind the village is a volcano that is alive and is smoking all the time. There is a lot of lava floating in the water, and it looks like floating rocks. The town of Kago Shima has 185,000 people, but we are about five miles from it. At the present we're about 100 miles southeast of Nagasaki, the town that was hit by the atomic bomb.

The weather here is swell. Almost the same as Minnesota this time of year. The temperature gets down to about 68 degrees at night and in the day time gets up to about 85.

Well, all for now.

Love, your son,

Don

P.S. I'm going to make that Motor Machinist Mate 1st class the first of the month.

Sept. 29, 1945

Dear Ellie:

This morning we got underway for Nagasaki. When we came in the mouth of the bay, we saw a shipyard and a lot of perty big freighters, partly built. In farther was a sunken tanker with just its bow and bridge out of water. As we came in farther we began to see the damage the fire bomb and atomic bomb raids had done. A lot of ships were sunk, and the frame work was all that was left of a lot of buildings. We passed another shipyard and saw where they were building two-man subs. There were a lot of them, but it looked like they had stopped work on them quite awhile ago.

We tied up to another tug, and from here we can see where the atomic bomb hit. It really flattened things out, and all the roofs of the buildings which are still standing are covered with junk. I've never seen anything like it!

The Japanese around here don't say anything or do anything... but I can imagine what they are thinking.

I don't know how long we will be around here, but it doesn't look as though we will leave for the states soon. I'm afraid we are stuck for awhile. All for now.

Love,

Don

UNITED STATES NAVY
RATING DESCRIPTION

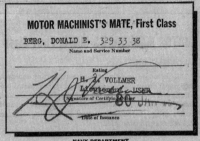

MOTOR MACHINIST'S MATE, First Class

BERG, DONALD E.   329 33 38
Name and Service Number

Rating

H. J. VOLLMER
Lieutenant, USNR
Signature of Certifying Officer

Date of Issuance

NAVY DEPARTMENT
BUREAU OF NAVAL PERSONNEL
NAVPERS 15257

UNITED STATES NAVY
RATING DESCRIPTION

TO THE VETERAN: *This Rating Description is an official document of the United States Navy. It has been issued to you mainly to help you get a job in civilian life which will make the best use of your naval training and experience. Don't hesitate to show it to any employer or prospective employer. Your Rating Description may prove to be one of your most valuable papers. Take care of it.*

MOTOR MACHINIST'S MATE, First Class

I. INTRODUCTION

This description is designed to give prospective employers, employment service officials, educators and other interested persons an over-all picture of the technical responsibilities assumed, duties performed, and knowledge and skills acquired by personnel in this rating. Representative related civilian occupations are included as a placement guide.

2

Oct. 2, 1945
Nagasaki

Dear Marg:

We're still here in Nagasaki sitting around doing nothing. A P.A. (passenger ship) came in yesterday that we were supposed to help tie up to a buoy, but they didn't need our help.

Last night we had the movie "Fighting Seabees", and I had to laugh at some parts of it like the Japs coming ashore in our landing barges and using our planes. Also, they were a lot fatter than the ones around here. Boy, I have never see skinnier people. It looks funny to see an American soldier on the beach with a lot of small Japanese all around.

I suppose you noticed by the envelope that I finally made 1st class. Now I draw $115 a month plus 20% for overseas time, so it comes out to around $138 a month which isn't too bad.

Is Herbert getting out this month? From what I hear over the radio, he should get out this month or next. Boy, I wish I could get my discharge now. We have sent quite a few guys back to the states for discharge, and with every-one that goes, he just drops a little more work on us. Perty soon we will be working over time. All for now.

Love,

Don

Oct. 6, 1945
Nagasaki

Dear Pop:

We're still here and nothing much has happened. One day we moved a Japanese sampan, and I got a chance to go aboard it. Most of the ship was perty crummy and covered with bugs and lice, so that when I got back aboard ship, I took a shower to make sure I didn't get any. I got a few things off of that wreck, and I'm enclosing a name plate off an electric motor.

The next day we got underway and went into the dock to make water. It was the first time we have tied up to a dock since we left Pearl. The seabees have Japanese harbor battalions working on the dock repairing it, and in a way they look funny. They don't know any modern methods, and the seabees have to show them how to do everything. The atomic bomb leveled a lot of the buildings, and now the Japs are clearing everything away.

We all got books on Japanese, and lately everyone has been trying to talk it, but it isn't too easy.

There is one theater about a block away that looks as though it was perty nice once. Now it isn't in too good of shape.

We still haven't received any mail, but a
"tin can" was supposed to bring some in last night,
so maybe we will get some today.
Well, chikai uchini omini kakari masu.
Love, your son,
Don

English	Pronunciation	Hepburn Spelling	Japanese Writing
Draw me a map! (*command*)	CHEE-zoo o KA-kay!	Chizu o kake!	地圖ヲ描ケ
I am an American	wa-TAHK-shee wa ah-may-ree-ka JEEN dess	Watakushi wa amerika jin desu	私ハアメリカ人デス
We are American soldiers	wa-ray-wa-ray wa ah-may-ree-ka no hay-ee-TA-ee DESS	Wareware wa amerika no heitai desu	我々ハアメリカノ兵隊デス
Are there soldiers near here?	chee-KA-koo nee hay-ee-TA-ee ga ee-MA-ska?	Chikaku ni heitai ga imasu ka?	近クニ兵隊ガ居マスカ
Where are they?	DOAK-o-nee ee-MA-ska?	Dokoni imasu ka?	何處ニ居マスカ
Are they our enemies?	KA-ray-ra wa tek-ee DESS-ka?	Karera wa teki desu ka?	彼等ハ敵デスカ
Where are American soldiers?	ah-may-ree-ka-no hay-ee-TA-ee wa DOAK-o-nee ee-MA-ska?	Amerika no heitai wa dokoni imasu ka?	アメリカノ兵隊ハ何處ニ居マスカ
How can I get there?	DOASS-oo-reb-ah so-ko-ay yoo-ka-ray MA-ska?	Dōsureba sokoe yukare masu ka?	如何スレバ其處ヘ行カレマスカ
Is there a train?	kee-SHA ga ar-ee-MA-ska?	Kisha ga arimasu ka?	汽車ガアリマスカ
Where is the station?	tay-ee-sha-ba w ka?		停車場ハ何處デスカ
Is there a bus?	BA-soo ga ah-re		
Where can I get the bus?	DOAK-o-day MA-ska?		
Please take me there	tsoo-ret-ay eet-		
Take me there! (*command*)	tsoo-ret-ay yoo		
You will be paid	ka-nay o ha-ra		
I want to eat	ta-bem-o-no o		

4
5

TM 30-641

RESTRICTED

JAPANESE
PHRASE BOOK

Dissemination of restricted matter. The information contained in restricted documents and the essential
characteristics of restricted material may be given to any
person known to be in the service of the United States
and to persons of undoubted loyalty and discretion who
are cooperating in Government work, but will not be
communicated to the public or to the press except by
authorized military public relations agencies. (See also
par. 18b, AR 380–5, 28 Sep 1942.)

WAR DEPARTMENT
WASHINGTON, FEBRUARY 28, 1944

Oct. 9, 1945
Nagasaki

Dear Mom:

We're still here in Nagasaki, and I guess we will be for quite awhile. When we first came into the dock, we got off the ship anytime, but now we have to have permission. Yesterday some of the guys went farther into town than they were supposed to, and the skipper didn't like it, so he clamped down. When we could get over, I got a few souvenirs. I'm enclosing a calendar and a fashion sheet so you can see the styles in Japan.

There is a mission here, and there were 16,000 Christians here before the atomic bomb hit. Now they have 8,000, but they are losing more everyday.

As yet we haven't had any mail, but every-day we have our hopes high until the mailman comes back and says no mail.

All for now.

Love, your son,
Don

Oct. 14, 1945
Nagasaki

Dear Ellie:

I made my first liberty the other day, and it wasn't much. Liberty started at 1:00 in the afternoon, so we got in an army duck and went to a government building to get our money changed into Japanese money. We got 15 yen for a dollar, and 100 sen for every yen. Right now I have a bundle of the stuff. From there we went downtown (that is if you could call it that) All there was was a lot of wooden shacks with a shop here and there. The people seemed friendly, and all the kids were saying "Konnichi wa" which means "Good afternoon". The women were fixing supper of raw chopped fish about the size of sardines,

Japanese soldiers

95

and it didn't look very inviting.

There weren't very many Japanese trucks around. Mostly there were horse or ox-drawn carts. A lot of the moving was done by hand though.

I went in a few shops, but they didn't have much...mostly Junk. I got one fairly nice cameo for 60 yen which is $4.00 in our money, and then I got a few pictures which I will enclose.

The Japanese have a police force that looks like a bunch of kids, but boy, they can be rough when they want to be. One day they caught a Jap trying to steal some army gear, and they kind of gave him a going over.

Liberty only lasted until 4:30, so when we got back, we all compared the things we had bought. It turned out to be mostly Junk.

I hope Mom still has those money order stubs. Last week a typhoon hit Okinawa again, and several ships were lost along with a lot of mail. So hang onto the stubs until I find out what the score is. All for now.

Love,

Don

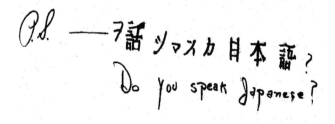

P.S. — ヲ話 シマスカ 日本 語?
Do you speak Japanese?

11
THE LONG WAIT FOR HOME

Another large typhoon struck in the area of Okinawa, and several tugs were called to help salvage ships which had been damaged or washed onto shore by the storm. After clean up, demobilization of the area began. Soldiers and sailors were sent home by the hundreds, and those who were left in the Pacific were anxious to see stateside orders or orders of discharge. There was also a concern among the many soldiers and sailors being discharged as to what civilian life might bring. Would there be jobs for them when they returned to the states?

Oct. 18, 1945
Okinawa

Dear Pop:

We are back in Okinawa and going to work. We're supposed to help salvage the ships that went on the beach here.

Two days ago we left Nagasaki for here, and on the way we had a little excitement. The lookouts spotted a floating Jap mine, so we loaded the guns and were going to explode it. We fired for about an hour at 800 yds., but we couldn't hit it. The sea was fairly rough, and it was starting to rain, so we reported the position by radio and went on again.

We got in here this morning, and boy is the beach ever a mess. All of Buckner Bay is covered with ships, and we are supposed to get them off. Some of them are up so far that there isn't a drop of water around the whole ship. I doubt if we will even try and get them off.

The other day we heard that the Navy is dropping its points, and it still doesn't do me any good. The way things look now, it will be March at least before I get out. Well, anyhow, I'll be able to get used to Minnesota weather starting in the spring time which is O.K. by me. Hey Pop, will you send me the sports sections of the Minnesota football games, so I can keep up on the dope?

All for now. Love, your son,

Don

Oct. 29, 1945
Okinawa

Dear Mom:

We're still here in Buckner Bay pulling ships off the beach. Since we got here, we have pulled an L.C.I. and a net tender off. The L.C.I. came off easy, but we really had to take a strain on the net tender. We pulled for 2 1/2 days at every high tide before she finally slid off the reef. The morning she came off, before we started to pull, I went over in the whaleboat with a 3 in. salvage pump in case they needed it. As soon as I got aboard, the "Mighty P" started to pull. At first the tender bounced forward a little, and then it began to slide off the reef. As we came off, the tender took a sharp port list, and I was almost afraid she might tip over. She didn't. Later on the crew put her on an even keel, and we put it along side a repair ship.

Today we got quite a bit of mail that was picked up on the beach after the typhoon hit here. My letter from Pop was so blurred that I could only read a few lines. It was dated the 23rd of Sept.

Boy, things are getting more unhappy every day out here. Ships are going out of the harbor with their homeward bound pennant flying, guys are getting transferred off her to go home, and here the "Mighty P" sits. As yet, the states are a long ways away for me.

Well, all for now.

Love, your son,
Don

November 24, 1945

Dear Ellie:

Boy, you don't know how hard this is getting to be to write letters. I'll sure be glad when I get back and don't have to write anymore.

Lately just about all the guys on here have been wondering what they are going to do when they get discharged, and I have been wondering myself. I'd like to have Pop or Herbert check over in Hopkins at the unemployment bu-

reau on the openings in diesel and refrigeration.
Like to get the dope on them, because I figure I
might start in that when I get out. I've had quite
a bit of work in both fields on here, and I think
one of them would be a good starter when I get
out. I've got other plans for later on, but right
now I've got to get in something to get started.
Right now I have hopes of getting some of that
free schooling in too. It will be nice to only have
to think about school.

Lately the engineering officer on here has
been trying to talk me into shipping over for a
couple more years, but as yet I can't see it. I'm
making perty fair money now, but I still like the
old outside better as yet. That is the reason I
want to find out how things stand for getting a
job back there, so I've got some idea of what I'm
getting into when I get my discharge.

We are back in Buckner Bay again, and
things are getting dark. Doesn't look like we are
going back yet. A lot of ships pulled out for the
states today, but we never get orders like that.
Sure hope we get those orders soon.

All for now, and I hope Pop will check on
that.

Your brother,

Don

P.S. Have you got anymore pictures? They
might bring back a few memories. Mom, here is

$40. If I do not get home for Christmas, please take the money and buy a gift for everyone.

Dec. 6, 1945
Buckner Bay

Dear Marg:

Well, we are still here, and will be for some time yet. Right now we are hooked up to an L.S.T. that was hit by a suicide plane and run up on the beach. Now we are going to pull it off and take it outside of the harbor and sink it. We pulled on it last night at high tide, but the other tug helping us broke their tow wire, so we secured. I guess we are going to pull again tonight.

Yesterday a Japanese cruiser came in here to get Jap prisoners and take them back to Japan. First time I've ever seen a Jap cruiser, and they don't look bad. They haven't too much fire power, but they look like they are perty fast. The Jap crew is still aboard and from what I could see through the field glasses, they looked perty crummy.

I received Pop's letter today saying something about buying a house out by Hopkins. Well, that sounds O.K. by me, and if he needs any of my money, that's O.K. too. I wish you would write and tell me all about this place, so I'll know what I will be coming back to and all that. Is there any water on the place?

I had a letter from John today too, and he seems to be doing all right at Norman. Surely hope he comes out all right in the Navy. Well, all for now.

Love,

Don

P.S. We are all a bunch of heroes, I guess, or so we have been telling each other. We made the hometown papers in the states. The Navy said we did a good job here on the Okinawa invasion and in salvaging the bow of the cruiser Pittsburgh.

Dec. 11, 1945

Dear Mom:

I'm glad to hear that you got the money for Christmas all right. Looks as though that is the best I can do this Christmas, because I know we can't make it back now.

The other day we got the L.S.T. off the beach and took it outside of the harbor and sank it. It had been hit by a suicide plane and was banged up in the typhoon too, so they figured it would be cheaper to sink it. An A.R.S. (Salvage ship) towed it out and when we were ten miles out, they dropped their tow wire and we opened fire on it with our 30 mm. and 40 mm. guns and had a lot of fun. We had a lot of ammo we wanted to get rid of, so we really did a lot of shooting. We fired at it for about a half hour or so and made a sieve out of it. Then she began to go down. She keeled over and went down bow first. As she went down, water shot out of the stern because of the air pressure inside, and then all of a sudden there was nothing left except a lot of bubbles.

From the letters we have been getting from the guys on here that have gone back for discharge, things must be tough as far as getting clothes and things like that. Is there anything I should try and get for us before I get my discharge? We might stop at Pearl Harbor. If and when we go back, I think we can get clothes there all right.

When you talk about cold weather, it makes me shiver. Why when it gets down to 55 degrees here, we think we are freezing to death.

I'm going to enclose some more negatives and you can get them developed if you want to.

Love, your son,

Don

December 21, 1945
4 days to Xmas

Dear Mom:

I'm now eligible for discharge the 1st of February according to the latest dope out. I've been thinking a lot about that too, and I've got my plans perty well worked out. If the ship stays out here, I'm going to get out as soon as I can, but if the "Mighty P" goes back to the states, I'm going to stay on here until about April. The way I look at it now, things don't look to good in the states for jobs, and I figure that by spring things should be a lot better.

After I get out I want to go through a refrigeration and then a business school if possible. After that I figure I'll be able to get into the refrigeration line O.K. I think I would get along best in that line. I would like to have someone check on the starting dates, so I will know how much time I've got after I get discharged. Also the length of time of the course.

How's chances of getting some pictures? I haven't gotten any for a long time. I'm going to forget how the place looks before long.

I want to wish everyone a Merry Christmas and Happy New Year, and hope I'll be able to be back for next Christmas!

Love, your son,

Don

Dec. 27, 1945
Okinawa

Dear Marg:

Guess it is about time I wrote to you. It's been kind of hard to write lately. This sitting around in here is just about driving me nuts.

Since demobilization started, we have lost quite a few men, and right now I'm acting chief in charge of the engineering gang. Since we have gotten short of men, it has been harder to keep up repairs, but it isn't too bad yet. Lately we have had quite a few jobs, and it's quite a job to get underway when we are short of men. As yet we haven't had too much trouble.

I'm enclosing a picture taken in Pearl last year that the Navy censor took away from us. It was just now returned. The picture had too much land in it, and the Navy figured they had better hold it until after the war. The other guy is J.B. Kopp of LA. Perty swell guy and we had a lot of good time together before he went back to the states for officer's training.

All for now, and maybe I'll see you soon.

Love,

Don

P.S. Where is my picture of you?

Jan. 2, 1946

Dear Mom:

Stop all my mail, cause I'm coming home! Yesterday I left the ship with some other guys and now we are on the island, sleeping in tents. Surely seems strange after being on the ship for better than two years. The aircraft carrier "Ticonderoga" is in here now and we figure on catching it so when you hear that it is back in the states, I should be there too. I should be in the states by the 20th and home before the 1st of Feb.

All for now.

Love, your son,
Don

Jan. 2

UNITED STATES NAVY

Dear Mom:

Stop all my mail, cause I'm
coming home! Yesterday I left
the ship with some other guys and
now we are on the island, sleeping
in tents. Surely seems strange
after being on the ship for better
than two years. The aircraft
carrier "Ticonderoga" is in here
now and we figure on catching
it so when you hear that it
is back in the states, I should
be there too. I should be in
the states by the 20th. and home
before the 1st. of Feb.
All for now.
                    Love, your son,
                            Don

To you who answered the call of your country and served in its Armed Forces to bring about the total defeat of the enemy, I extend the heartfelt thanks of a grateful Nation. As one of the Nation's finest, you undertook the most severe task one can be called upon to perform. Because you demonstrated the fortitude, resourcefulness and calm judgment necessary to carry out that task, we now look to you for leadership and example in further exalting our country in peace.

Harry Truman

THE WHITE HOUSE

OFFICE OF
THE ADMINISTRATOR OF
VETERANS AFFAIRS

DEAR FELLOW VETER

I congratul
the armed forces
a two-front war
of the Axis Powe

Having been appointed by the Presiden
of Veterans Affairs, I want to state generally the provisi
made by our Government for you and other veterans.

Among the benefits that you may be entitled to are compensation for disabilities, hospitalization, home, farm and business loan guarantee, readjustment allowances, insurance, rehabilitation and vocational training, educational courses, assistance in obtaining employment and provision for your dependents.

Eligibility for each one is dependent upon the facts in the individual case.

If you are interested in any of these provisions, you should write or contact the Veterans Administration office nearest your home. For your convenience, there is, on the reverse of this letter, a list of the Regional Offices with the address of each office.

I feel I should warn you the last deduction for your Government insurance premiums has been made from your service pay. This means from now on you must make these premium payments directly to the Collections division, Veterans Administration, Washington 25, D. C.

DON'T LET YOUR INSURANCE LAPSE! YOU
OWE THIS TO YOURSELF AND YOUR FAMILY.

I assure you that the Veterans Administration stands ready to serve you.

Sincerely yours,

Omar N. Bradley

OMAR N. BRADLEY,
General, U. S. Army.
Administrator.

EPILOGUE

Donald Berg was separated from active duty in the United States Navy on January 30, 1946. He returned to Minneapolis, Minnesota, separation center, where he was honorably discharged. After a wonderful reunion with his family, he took on the task of looking for that job that he had on his mind for so many months. His experience with diesel engines paid off for him as he was able to get his first civilian job working on diesel engines.

On June 28, 1947, Don married Cecile Peterson, and in the same year, he took a new job in the brand new field of computer technology. He became a serviceman for Burroughs Computers and continued with the company (later to become Unisys) until he retired as a service manager in 1985. His wife and he had two children, Susan in 1949 and James in 1951.

Donald attended several USS *Pakana* reunions in the 1980s and early 1990s. They were wonderful times of renewed friendships and reminiscing. He did not know until the reunions that he had returned on the USS *Ticonderoga* with one of his buddies. The ship was so large that they never saw each other.

On June 24, 1996, Donald Berg died at his home surrounded by those he loved. His joys in life were his wife, his children and their spouses, his grandchildren, his faith, gardening, ice cream, pictures, and laughter. He wrote very few letters after he returned from the Pacific, but he continued to appreciate the simple moments in life.

Don and daughter Susan, Memorial Day 1950

WORLD WAR II TIME LINE

1939

September 1, 1939:	Germany invades Poland.
September 3, 1939:	Britain and France declare war on Germany.
November 30, 1939:	Russia invades Finland.

1940

May 10, 1940:	Germany invades Holland, Belgium, and Luxembourg.
September 27, 1940:	Japan joins the Axis.

1941

June 22, 1941:	Germany invades Russia.
December 7, 1941:	Japan attacks Pearl Harbor.
December 8, 1941:	The U.S. declares war on Japan.
December 10, 1941:	Japan begins invasion of the Philippines.
December 11, 1941:	Germany and Italy declare war on the U.S.; Japan invades Guam.

1942

April 9, 1942:	U.S. forces surrender at Bataan, the Philippines, and the Bataan Death March begins.
May 1942:	Sugar is rationed in the U.S.
June 3-7, 1942:	Battle of Midway, Japan's first major defeat.

August 7, 1942:	U.S. troops land on Guadalcanal.
December 1942:	Rationing of gasoline begins in all U.S. states.

1943

March 29, 1943:	Meat rationing begins in the U.S.
July 25, 1943:	Mussolini is deposed.
September 3, 1943:	Italy surrenders to the Allies.

1944

February 1944:	Battle for Kwajalein.
June 6, 1944:	D-Day. Thousands of British, American, and Canadian troops land at Normandy and begin the invasion of Western Europe.
June 15, 1944:	Battle for Saipan.
July 20, 1944:	U.S. troops land on Guam.
August 24, 1944:	Allies liberate Paris.
October 20, 1944:	U.S. forces land at Leyte in the Philippines.
December 16, 1944:	The last major German counteroffensive begins in the Ardennes; Battle of the Bulge.

1945

February 4, 1945:	Manila, Philippines, liberated.
February 19 - March 15, 1945:	Battle of Iwo Jima.

April 1 - **June 22, 1945:**	Battle of Okinawa.
April 12, 1945:	Roosevelt dies; Harry S. Truman becomes president.
April 28, 1945:	Mussolini is executed.
April 30, 1945:	Hitler commits suicide.
April 1 - **June 22, 1945:**	Battle of Okinawa.
May 7, 1945:	Germany surrenders unconditionally.
May 8, 1945:	V-E Day. Allies declare victory in Europe.
August 6, 1945:	U.S. drops atomic bomb on Hiroshima, Japan.
August 9, 1945:	U.S. drops atomic bomb on Nagasaki, Japan.
August 14, 1945:	V-J Day. Japan surrenders.
September 2, 1945:	Japan signs surrender agreement on the USS *Missouri* anchored in Tokyo Bay.

GLOSSARY

allotment: A portion of a sailor's pay that is regularly deducted for the sailor's dependents, for savings, or for insurance.

barracks: Buildings used to house military personnel.

BM: Boatsman Mate.

bow: The front end of a ship.

bumming: Borrowing.

cabbage: Money.

Cat Fever: Bronchial pneumonia.

colors: A flag ceremony.

company: A group of sailors under the command of a Chief Petty Officer.

convoy: A group of ships traveling together for safety.

CPO: Chief Petty Officer.

demobilization: The act of discharging sailors from military service, sending them home.

discharge: To release someone from military service.

dope: News or information.

even keel: A stable position.

fall in for inspection: To get in line to be inspected by an officer for neatness and completion of uniform and neatness of surroundings.

fish: A torpedo.

GI: Government issue; also a term used for military personnel.

GI can: A government issue trash can.

GQ: General Quarters; orders to be prepared for battle.

gate: Golden Gate Bridge in San Francisco, California.

getting it in the neck: Getting in trouble.

gold braid: An officer.

hooks: Golf clubs.

ID tag: An identification tag worn around the neck which states name and rank in the military; also called dog tags.

LCT: Landing craft tank.

liberty: Free time away from the ship or base.

list: When a ship leans to one side.

LST: Landing ship tank.

MAA: Master at Arms.

mess hall: The building where meals are served.

MoMM1/c: Motor Machinist Mate 1st Class.

MoMM2: Motor Machinist Mate 2nd Class.

net tender: A naval vessel that opened and closed a gate of cables which were woven together like a net to keep submarines out of a harbor area.

port: The left side of a ship.

quarantined: isolated to prevent the spread of a contagious disease.

rationing: The practice of limiting the purchase of food or other supplies during wartime, often using ration coupons.

sack: Bed.

semaphore: A visual system of signaling with two flags which are held one in each hand. Letters of the alphabet are represented by different positions of the arms and flags.

sentry: A guard posted in a position to prevent unauthorized persons from passing.

short: Not having enough of a particular item.

small stores: A store on the naval base for the purchase of clothing or small supplies.

stand watch: To stand guard.

states: The United States of America.

strafing: A low-flying aircraft attacking with its machine gun firing.

strictly GI: Strictly following the rules of the military.

swell: Super, great, wonderful, cool.

take the town apart: Celebrate.

tin can: A small navy vessel; a destroyer.

topside: On the upper deck of a ship.

USO: United Service Organization. An organization devoted to entertainment and help for US military personnel.

wolf: A girl popular with the boys or a boy popular with the girls.

work detail: Work assignment.

BIBLIOGRAPHY

Becton, Rear Admiral F. Julian, USN,Ret. and Morschauser, Joseph III. The Ship that Would Not Die. Missoula, Montana, Pictorial Histories Company, 1980.

Berg, Donald E. "Ship's History - U.S.S. Pakana (ATF 108)"

Bobick, Chet. "Capture of Okinawa Gunto, 3-25-45 to 6-8-45."

BoomerWeb.net Communities 2000. "War Rationing - Welcome to 1942."
   http://www.boomerweb.net/livingretro/rationing/index.html
   (viewed 2-18-02)

Clancey, Patrick. "Ships of the U.S. Navy, 1940-1945."
   http://www.sunsite.unc.edu/hyperwar/USN/USN-ships.html
   (viewed 6-16-98)

Esposito, Vincent J. "The War in the Southern and Southwestern Pacific."
   http://www.gi.grolier.com/wwii_9.html (viewed 6-16-98)

"Famous People and Glossary."
   http://www.users.bergen.org/~jacput/people.htm
   (viewed 6-17-98)

Guttman, Robert. "Fleet Battered by Typhoon." World War II, 9: 26-32,77, Jan. 1995.

Harper, Dale P. "U.S.S. Laffey's Pacific Ordeal."
   http://www.the historynet.com/WorldWarII/articles/1998 /0398_text.htm   (viewed 3-20-98)

Hayes, John D. "Developments in Naval Warfare."
   http://www.gi.grolier.com/wwii_12.html (viewed 6-17-98)

Hayes, John D. "The War in the Central and Northern Pacific."
   http://www.gi.grolier.com/wwii_10.html (viewed 6-17-98)

Hitchcock, Jane A. and Christopher N. "Battle of Okinawa
    Statistics."
    http://www.geocities.com/~hitchcockc/okibattle.html
    (viewed 6-17-98)

McCracken, Carolyn. "Enola Gay Perspectives: The War in the
    Pacific." Group project within the course LBSC 791 (Spring
    1995) in the College of Library and Information Services at
    the U. of Maryland, College Park.
    http://www.glue.umd.edu/~enola/hist/history.html
    (viewed 6-17-98)

Microsoft Corporation. Microsoft Bookshelf '94 CD Rom for
    Macintosh. Microsoft Corporation, 1994.

Military History Forum. "Battles of Iwo Jima and Okinawa."
    http://www.militaryhistory@aol.com

Naval Historical Center. "Traditions of Our Naval Heritage."
    http://www.history.navy.mil/nhc11.htm
    (viewed 6-16-98)

O'Grady Kathy. "What Did You Do in the War, Grandma?"
    http://www.stg.brown.edu/projects/WWII_Women/NewTime
    line.html#1943 (viewed 2-18-02)

"The Story of WWII." Grolier Online, 1999.
    http://www.gi.grolier.com/wwii (viewed 2-18-02)

Wadsworth, Kent. "'Tin Can' Odyssey." The American Legion
    Magazine, 141:24-25,46-47, Dec. 1996.

"World War II," The New Grolier Multimedia Encyclopedia,
    Release 6 CD Rom for Macintosh. Grolier Inc., 1993.